W9-CFZ-854

ideals
MOTHER'S DAY

A mother's love
Is indeed the golden link
That binds youth to age;
And he is still but a child,
However time may have
Furrowed his cheek,
Or silvered his brow,
Who can yet recall,
With a softened heart,
The fond devotion
Or the gentle chidings
Of the best friend
That God ever gives us.

Bovee

ISBN 0-8249-1002-8 350

IDEALS—Vol. 38, No. 3 April MCMLXXXI. IDEALS (ISSN 0019-137X) is published eight times a year,
January, February, April, June, July, September, October, November
by IDEALS PUBLISHING CORPORATION, 11315 Watertown Plank Road, Milwaukee, Wis. 53226
Second class postage paid at Milwaukee, Wisconsin. Copyright © MCMLXXXI by IDEALS PUBLISHING CORPORATION.
Postmaster, please send form 3579 to Ideals Publishing Corporation, Post Office Box 2100, Milwaukee, Wis. 53201
All rights reserved. Title IDEALS registered U.S. Patent Office.
Published simultaneously in Canada.

ONE-YEAR SUBSCRIPTION—eight consecutive issues as published—$15.95
TWO-YEAR SUBSCRIPTION—sixteen consecutive issues as published—$27.95
SINGLE ISSUES—$3.50

Publisher, James A. Kuse
Managing Editor, Ralph Luedtke
Editor/Ideals, Colleen Callahan Gonring
Associate Editor, Linda Robinson
Production Manager, Mark Brunner
Photographic Editor, Gerald Koser
Copy Editor, Norma Barnes
Art Editor, Duane Weaver

What Would You Call a Most Delicate Thing?

Elsie Pearson

What would you call a most delicate thing?
Is it the touch of a butterfly's wing?
Is it a birdsong so silver and free,
Dew-spangled spider web caught on a tree?
What would you call a most delicate thing?

Is it the pale pastel blue of the sky?
Cotton-wool scrap of a cloud floating by?
Is it the touch of a lover-like hand?
Shimmering moonlight on smooth silver sand?
What would you call a most delicate thing?

Scrap of humanity, ribbons and lace,
Tiny curled fingers, and wee wrinkled face,
Pink puckered mouth like a velvety rose.
Sleepy blue eyes and the teeniest nose.
Here on a downy head, soft as a prayer.
One tiny ringlet of soft golden hair . . .
That's what I call a most delicate thing.

The Bornin' Room

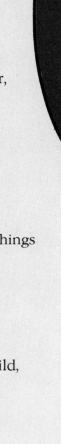

The little room adjoined
the Keeping Room,
A special room with
linens laid away,
Kept spic and span;
upon the old handloom,
A coverlet was woven
for the day
When the room would
proudly welcome there
A little babe; this was
the Bornin' Room.
The pumpkin pine chest,
dovetailed, mellowed, fair,
Held treasure in its
faintly scented gloom.
Woolen garments from
the sheeps' wool spun,
And woven into cloth
warm and strong
From flax that ripened
in the summer sun,
Were fashioned in baby things
that lasted long.
The fireplace held logs
so neatly piled,
The flint and tinder
ever ready near.
And, though the winds
outside were cold and wild,
The little room would
glow with rosy cheer,
To keep the newborn
and its mother warm.
When all was over,
peace dwelt in the gloom.
The house abustle—
here lay a certain calm
Like benediction
in the Bornin' Room.

Ruth B. Field

Portrait of My Mother

Mother's hands weave carefully,
Carefully and well,
Warp and weft of human life
Patterned to excel.
Happily they persevere,
All the while believing
In the tapestry of love
That they are achieving.
Hands that labor thus accrue
Beauty that is mother's due.

Lydia O. Jackson

She smiles as her needle goes in and out;
Her thoughts dance merrily—whirl about,
Glowing—

Glowing with love for her daughters four
Whom God has sent through her heart's great door.

She stitches some squares for a patchwork quilt;
The squares, like her life, are sturdily built.

The patches are bits of aprons and frocks,
Reminding her keenly of falls and knocks,

Of school days and questions to solve mysteries,
Of gay fudge parties and banged-up knees.

A little thing in stature—but still
A giant in courage and strength of will.

Facing the years as a grandmother—kind!
With new lives to love, new wounds to bind.

She is my mother.

Doris A. Paul

Carice Williams

A Happy Home

A happy home's a jewel box
More dear than rubies rare.
Contentment reigns in every room,
For love is present there.

Laughter and tears and work and play
Are shared together here,
And family prayers are also heard
Within these walls so dear.

No wonder that these family ties
Grow stronger every day,
For sharing's like a lantern bright
Which lights a darkened way.

Born and raised in Chicago, Illinois, Carice Williams has been writing poetry since her teens. Her poetry first appeared in *Ideals* in 1959. Over the years, her work has been published in the *Chicago Tribune* and broadcast regularly over local Chicago radio stations. Miss Williams' poems have not only been widely read in the United States, but have been accepted in England, Wales, and Japan. Other activities that Miss Williams enjoys include needlepoint, gardening, cooking, photography, and traveling. Among her many honors, she has received the Masonic Coin Award in 1966 for her poetic contributions to their publications. Her two books, *Echoes from the Heart* and *Doorway to Dreams,* provide continuing inspiration for many readers today.

Old-Fashioned Garden

I love an old-fashioned garden
With violets, dainty and grand,
And borders of gentle alyssum
Like a carpet of snow on the land.

I love an old-fashioned garden
With hollyhocks, stately and tall,
And soft little pansies, like velvet,
Lined up by an old garden wall.

The jack-in-the-pulpit and larkspurs,
The lilies and soft Queen Anne's lace
Transform, as by magic, my garden
To a sweet little old-fashioned place.

Happiness

It's happiness when I can feel
The warmness of the sun,
Some flowers round my kitchen door
(I treasure everyone),
The silver of the moonbeams' rays
That light the sky at night,
The many little twinkling stars
That shine so very bright.

It's happiness for me to hear
A songbird's sweet refrain
Or smell the lilac's fragrant blooms
After a soft spring rain.
To capture all these lovely things
Whenever they come my way
Gives me a feeling of great joy
And love to fill my day.

Mother Love

You can't define a mother's love:
It's faith and hope and power.
It's wisdom and unselfishness,
Protection hour by hour.

You can't define a mother's love:
It's prayers, true and sincere,
It's tenderness and sympathy,
A smile, a dream, a tear.

You can't define a mother's love:
It's faith that never grows dim.
And through a mother's love is found
The path that leads to Him.

Mother

Mother, only Mother,
Is like a candle bright,
That keeps its flame aglowing
Throughout the darkest night.

Mother's love is changeless,
And never does she tire,
For each day she's fulfilling
All that our needs require.

Mother, only Mother,
Was sent by Heaven above
To fill our hearts with gladness,
With tenderness and love.

Appreciation

It's the little things in life that count,
Which make it worth the while,
The laughter of a little child,
A loving mother's smile.

A welcome mat outside the door,
A few friends in for tea,
Two chairs beside a fireplace
That wait for you and me.

One can't appraise the value
Of the things we see each day
We have to know and live them
As we travel on life's way.

The things we work the hardest for
We cherish all the more.
We search afar for happiness
When it's just outside our door.

Mother's Wisdom

"You are what you think,"
My mother would say,
As she spoke words of wisdom
For work and for play.
"Think mean, and you'll surely
Turn out to be mean.
Have thoughts that are pure,
And your mind will be clean."

I've tried to remember
While traveling life's way
The wisdom that Mother
Would use in her day.
It's still just as sound
As a chain's strongest link:
"Remember, my child,
You are what you think."

In the intricately beautiful world of sculptured porcelain art, Cybis is a name synonymous with old-world quality and elegance. Although reminiscent of the painstakingly hand-fashioned porcelains produced in the old Saxony region of eastern Europe, Cybis sculptures in America originated in the unlikely place of Astoria, New York. Today, the Cybis Studio occupies a converted carriage house in Trenton, New Jersey. Here its many artists carry on the work of the studio's founder, Boleslaw Cybis, a man of enormous artistic talents. The legend of this creative genius is as enduring as the porcelains which continue to emerge from the kilns he built.

Boleslaw Cybis was born in Poland, the son of the chief architect who designed the Czarina Maria Fiodorovna's summer palace in Moscow. While Cybis was an art student at the St. Petersburg Academy of Fine Arts in Russia, the revolution erupted, forcing him to flee to Constantinople. The young artist scratched out a living sketching portraits in outdoor cafes and fashioning unusual clay pipes which, he was surprised to learn, soon became popular collectors' items.

Eventually, Cybis returned to Warsaw and enrolled in the Academy of Fine Arts. There he organized a group of artists dedicated to studying the techniques of the old masters, denying the modernistic trends of the time. In 1925, he graduated and, a year later, married Marja Tym, a talented fellow art student at the Academy. After years of traveling and studying throughout Europe and Africa, Cybis returned to Poland, where he was appointed a professor at the Warsaw Academy in 1937.

In 1938, the Polish government commissioned Cybis and his wife, Marja, an accomplished artist in her own right, to paint murals in the Hall of Honor in the Polish Pavilion at the World's Fair in the United States. A year later when their project was completed, the couple tried to return to Poland, but their ship was forced to turn around in mid-Atlantic when World War II began. They returned to the United States and decided to establish an artists' studio like the one they had left behind in Poland. Taking over the Steinway Mansion in Astoria, New York, they began working in a variety of media. The couple invited other artists to join them and acquired the talents of an exceptional ceramic art student, Marylin Kozuch, also of Polish descent.

Noticing the lack of porcelain studios in America, the Cybises decided to establish Cybis Art Productions to create the same fine porcelain sculptures they had known in the region of their birth. Seeking larger kilns and more artists familiar with the complexities of porcelain sculpture, the Cybises moved their studio to Trenton, New Jersey, where a large number of ceramic studios already existed.

Creating delicate porcelain art requires the talents of many artists who must work together like a finely rehearsed orchestra wishing to create a beautiful symphony. Porcelain is made from a clay mix that is silky smooth and able to remain in suspension. Delicate brushes and fine dental tools are used to shape the clay. Molds are used for large figurines, but the final shaping is always done by hand. When the composition is ready for firing, the parts seem to be at an awkward angle. As slow heat flows through the kiln, the clay mixture settles and the sculptures take their correct positions. Porcelain must cool slowly, and since moisture trapped inside can cause it to explode, each porcelain is vented. Cybis frequently uses a tiny pin prick in a concealed place on the sculpture. Because of the intense heat inside the kiln, colors must be of metallic content and are of endless variations.

Before Boleslaw and Marja Cybis died in 1957 and 1958, their studio had gained a wide reputation for excellence in the field of porcelain art. Today, the traditions of Cybis porcelains have been kept alive through the leadership of Marylin Kozuch, who later became Marylin Chorlton, and her husband, Joseph. Many of the original artists are still with the Cybis Studio, carrying on brilliant, imaginative work and training others to succeed them in future generations.

Cybis sculptures are valued by art collectors throughout the world, being found in such prestigious residences as Buckingham Palace, the White House, and the Vatican. Visiting dignitaries to Washington, D.C., can view the entire Cybis North American Indian Series on display at Blair House, the nation's official guest house. One of this collection's most beautiful pieces is "Sacajawea," the sculpture of a Shoshone squaw of legendary courage. Halfway across the world rests another famous, although fictional, female character cast in porcelain. Princess Aurora from the ballet *Sleeping Beauty*, along with her handsome Prince Florimund, are delicately poised in Russia's Bolshoi Choreography School. These figurines were gifts from the United States to the Bolshoi Ballet in 1972.

Serving as special ambassadors for the American people, Cybis sculptures have been frequently presented as Gifts of State by the White House. Queen Elizabeth II was presented with The Colonial Flower Basket during her Bicentennial visit to the United States. The outstanding Presidential Chess Set was given to the Soviet Union during the 1972 Moscow Summit Conference. Pope John Paul II received The Bride during his historical tour of the United States.

In this day of mass production and rapid automation, Americans can take pride in the elegant old-world art form that has taken root in this country. The mystique of Cybis porcelain sculptures can be captured in the words of one of history's most notable collectors, the Polish king, Augustus the Strong, who said porcelain was "like the fruit of the exotic orange; given a taste for one, you'll never have enough."

Michele Arrieh

Circle
of Love

Kate Douglas Wiggin

In a true family circle a father and a mother first clasp each other's hands, liking well to be thus clasped; then they stretch out a hand on either side, and these are speedily grasped by children, who hold one another firmly and complete the ring. The minute that two, three, four, five join in, the roundness grows, and the merriment, too, and the laughter and the power to do things—a family circle round and complete, with love and harmony between all its component parts.

Ofttimes across the room you come
To press a kiss against my hair,
To hold me for no cause at all,
Save love. At once our small ones there
Come laughing, making a ring-around.
So does devotion strike a spark
That showers into golden light,
Gathering children in its arc.

Virginia Moody Hagan

On the Wings of Night

On the wings of the night, I passed
The house where I first wept and laughed,
And felt the wind on meadow grass
In the clarity of morning,
When hills were lilac blossoms stacked,
And hurts were mended by a kiss,
And hopes were bright as daisy chains,
And dreams, a singing of flamebirds,
And love, a tender sheltering
Neath a star in the crib window.
But, ah, now I cannot tarry,
My heart's beating too busy fast
For that wonder in the dawning
Of joy new as the early dew—
Only the astonished glimpse back
As I hasten, hasten onward.
Poor wayworn pilgrim—be dazzled!
There is still time—aye, dear, still time . . .

Mary Roelofs Stott

The Watcher

She always leaned to watch for us,
  Anxious if we were late,
In winter by the window,
  In summer by the gate.

And though we mocked her tenderly,
  Who had such foolish care,
The long way home would seem more safe
Because she waited there.

Her thoughts were all so full for us,
  She never could forget!
And so I think that where she is
  She must be watching yet,

Waiting till we come home to her,
  Anxious if we are late—
Watching from heaven's window,
  Leaning from heaven's gate.

Margaret Widdemer

Beadwork—The elegant adornment in fashion history

Since the days of the Pharaohs, beadwork has been used for adornment. Fashioned from many stones and of various shapings, it was used profusely by both women and men. Pictures painted on ancient walls show figures wearing gold-beaded girdles and deep, flat collars of innumerable rows of rich beads, with pendants of beads covering the breast like a mantilla. In classical Greece, fashionable ladies gave great attention to their hair arrangements, and as a final touch added strands of beads, enameled with gold.

Beads of brass, jet, and amber have survived the climatic conditions of the tombs of first century Northern Europeans. The bodice of the Medieval costume sparkled with its bead covering, and the French Renaissance gown was likely to be detailed and edged with gold beads.

But it remained for dress of the Victorian Era to carry elaborate beadwork to the extreme. The lavish ornamentation that gave form and character to costume of the day was characterized by beaded fringe, beaded garniture, medallion-shaped appliques of beads, braid, and buttons; and beaded passementerie, a mixing of beads and braids. Beadwork appeared everywhere, even on articles for outdoor wear. Mantles and capes were embellished. Jackets were constructed totally of bronze, steel or jet beading worked into netting.

The wide shoulders of the Gay Nineties were emphasized by lovely bead garnitures. Crystal beads sometimes were used on the tailored suit and dress. After the turn of the century, French influence was seen on black dresses made more elegant with white beading. Later, artistic beading ornamented otherwise simple blouses and frocks.

The Flapper Age dress, a short, straight silhouette, was enhanced by such attractive decoration. Extravagantly covered with beading, some attained weights up to twelve pounds. Bugle bead trim was found on many of the glamorous bias-cut dresses of the 1930s. And the evening sweater was beautified with gold and silver beads.

Trailing floral-pattern bead appliques accented the fitted 1940s stylings. Elaborate beading effects, which came to include plastic beads, continued to be popular into the second half of the twentieth century. They were evident, not only on dresses, but also on the very popular chiffon-lined sweater.

Throughout fashion history these shiny little perforated balls also have been very much a part of the dress accessory. During the time of Louis IV, the beaded, crocheted and/or knitted bag appeared, and in the Victorian Era there was a great variety of shapes and fastenings. In the early years, bags of fine seedlike beads were closely netted into elaborate patterns to resemble those of the late 1600s. Also fashionable were dark blue or black velvet bags embroidered with steel or gilt beads.

Characteristic of this age was the "long purse." These bags were of crocheted or knitted netting made into narrow tubes; they were silk-lined and usually beaded. A beaded tassel was attached at one end and beaded openwork at the other. Beads were sometimes worked into the mesh to give a dew-spangled effect. Other examples were netted more closely so that only the beads were visible. More commonly known as stocking or miser purses, they were carried by both men and women.

Smart leather purses of the early 1900s were richly ornamented with multi-shaped and -sized jet beading; the very finely beaded bag, exquisite in color and design, was the 1918 mode. Small, fancily beaded clutch bags continued to be stylish in the 1930s and the 1950s.

Fashion attention also was given to the bead-embossed belt. This adornment was worn by men of the sixteenth century and later by wasp-waisted ladies of the Nineties. Together with the beaded, tasseled sash, these belts were popular accessories in the Roaring Twenties.

Beaded jewelry has been popular throughout the years. Bracelets, broaches, earrings, and rings were fashioned from beads. Neckbands have been made from interlaced beading. In Renaissance England, both sexes wore necklaces. As early as 1800, beaded chains were twisted about the neck six or seven times. Wearing a variety of bead necklaces of different lengths at the same time was stylish before and after 1920. "Ropes" of beads, especially cascades of black beads, were also an important part of the Twenties fashion scene.

Topping the total fashion look was the 1860 jet-trimmed bonnet and bead-sprinkled net cowl worn over the chignon, the 1870 hat and bonnet whose elaborate ornamentation is accented by steel, bronze or jet beads. Buckles of these kinds of beads were the vogue during the turn of the century's "gilded age." All-over glitter can be noted on the 1950 beaded calot worn for evening occasions. Hat pins are strikingly decorative and most beautiful topped with beads used singularly or in clusters.

Fashion history details the popularity of beading in all areas of hair-dressing. Tiaras, many-styled combs, and other adornments were made more elaborate by the use of beading.

In the past, beads have also been used to strikingly ornament the home. In the late 1800s they decorated picture frames and pin cushions, and formed table covers, draperies and fireside screens. Lamp shades were edged with beaded fringe. Long strands of wood and/or plastic beads used in doorways and windows were a style of the early 1970s.

Instruction books have been readily available through the years for all kinds of needlework, including Indian beadwork. Garnitures, passementeries, fringe and other miscellaneous bead trims were also made available, from mail-order catalogs, through which they were sold by the yard or by the piece.

Throughout fashion history, beadwork has added a touch of elegance to clothing, accessories, and household furnishings.

Loraine B. Lobotzky and Tom Sersha

Peter's Poem

Lee Bock

One sunny Monday, Peter Michael McStone
Stood by some bookshelves in his home.
    The bookshelves were tall, much taller than he,
    Which made it quite difficult for him to see
What was sitting on top of the very top shelf.
That's when he decided, "I'll see for myself!
    I won't tell anyone what I have in mind,
    And maybe I'll find something I shouldn't find!"

Peter Michael McStone thought hard for a minute.
He looked round the room to see what was in it:
    "I'll have to have something to stand on, I suppose,
    So my feet will be up where my nose usually goes."
First he stacked four pillows on his rocking chair,
Stood on top of the pile, his arms waving in air.
    But the chair rocked and rocked, and then rocked some more,
    Till Peter Michael McStone fell plop on the floor.

Before very long he had one more idea,
But he needed some help, so he yelled, "Oh, Maria!
    Will you come over here to help me for a while?
    And get down on your knees?" he asked with a smile.
Well, his sister did, but she soon gave a yell
When he stood on her back—and, kerplunk, down he fell!

There on the floor he thought to himself
Of another plan to see that top shelf:
    "No one is better at building than I!
    I can pile my blocks clear up to the sky—
Or at least to the ceiling," he said with a giggle,
And he danced round the floor with two leaps and one wiggle.
    Peter Michael McStone stacked the blocks one, two, three;
    The building grew taller, right up to his knee,
And then to his hips, his waist, and his shoulder.
Peter Michael McStone grew bolder and bolder.
    To his nose, his eyelashes, forehead, and hair,
    And over his head! But he couldn't stop there:
"It has to be taller than ever before!"
At last when it reached to the top of the door
    He climbed right up on that special block home.
    But it all fell down on Peter Michael McStone.

It was not very long before he knew
Of still another plan that he could do:
    "I think I can climb up the side, shelf by shelf,
    Right up to the top to see for myself!"
So slowly and carefully, he climbed up and up
And just as he got his nose to the top,
    His mother said, "Peter Michael McStone,
    Come down here this minute!" He wasn't alone.
His mother said, "Son, I wish that I knew
What in the world's the matter with you!"

But Peter Michael McStone kept his thoughts to himself,
Planning a new way to see that top shelf.
    He thought so hard that his face got all crumpled,
    He rubbed his chin, and his eyebrows got rumpled.
"My last plan will work, and that's very plain:
I will tape a mirror to my grandfather's cane!"
    Soon he held the cane high, beside the top shelf,
    And just like that, he could see for himself!

Do you want me to tell you? I suppose that I must:
What Peter Michael McStone saw was nothing but dust.

Faces

Faces that I have loved return to me
As easily, sometimes, from long ago
As yesterday: I close my eyes and see
Young playmates' faces laughing in the snow,
And favorite teachers' faces, and the kind
Faces of old folk, soft and many-lined.

There's the adoring face of my first love,
And those of friends forever lost to view,
And, very dear, my mother's face above
Her work, or smiling all the smiles we knew—
While finely sensitive, yet strangely strong,
Your face is never absent from me long.

And there is many a time and many a place
It seems I almost look upon God's face.

Elaine V. Emans

Old Photographs

A box of faded photographs
I opened yesterday,
And instantly my memories
Were carried far away

To many friends and places
From years so long ago,
As I sorted through those photographs
Of folks I used to know.

There were some of family members
That are no longer here,
And photographs of sweethearts
I once thought very dear.

Thoughts swiftly raced and tumbled
On things that are no more,
As I daydreamed over photographs
And happy days of yore.

Ernest Jack Sharpe

The Divine Flower

Because the strength of our country so often lies in the hands of the women who quietly train their children in "the way that they should go," a salute to motherhood is always appropriate. In recognition of these women, a flower was selected for Mother's Day that is called "The Divine Flower" (Dianthus), known to us as the carnation or clover pink.

Nearly three-hundred species of *Dianthus* are found throughout southern Euro-Asia, especially in France and northern Italy. Over a period of at least five centuries, European horticulturists developed the present garden and florist species by means of selection and hybridization. Most carnations originated from *Dianthus caryophyllus*, which was known and described by Theophatus as early as 300 B.C. This attractive wild plant, with its small, single, white flowers, had often been crossbred with other *Dianthus*, particularly *D. chinensis*, to give us the many attractive strains which are available today. Carnations have remained popular garden and florist flowers since the sixteenth century when they were the principal flowers of the English garden.

The carnation continues to be a popular garden flower in America, though it does have weaknesses which must be considered. Theoretically a perennial, it is not hardy in regions of severe frost and ice, such as the Midwest and New England. Carnations should generally be considered annuals, or at best biennials north of Washington, D.C.; however, if given a protective mulch of loose, free-draining material, some may survive in colder areas. Abundant sunlight is essential and soil must be non-acid and only moderately rich.

Despite these limitations, carnations are excellent garden flowers, having interesting and colorful blooms, a long flowering period with numerous flowers, and an excellent fragrance. The bluish-gray foliage contrasts distinctively with other vegetation. Few other flowers offer as much bloom and fragrance. The doubled flowers range in color from red, scarlet, pink and white to purple and yellow. Some have a single hue, some are striped, and others are edged with contrasting colors. They vary in height from ten to twenty inches, including erect dwarf varieties and willowy taller types that may need staking.

Many parts of our country are, at one time or another, too hot, too cold, or too wet for desired success, but northern dwellers can enjoy carnations as annuals, southerners, as early flowering perennials. In mid-America they may grow vigorously where summers are mild and winter mulching is practiced. The cooler coastal areas should have the best results, provided lime is available in well-drained soil. Carnations can be compared to hardy mums in durability and reliability.

Although carnations can be seeded directly into the garden, they may not develop fully enough in northern climates to bloom well the first year. Plants can either be purchased in pots in spring or be homegrown. Seeds should be sown indoors or in cold frames six to eight weeks before outdoor planting. Young plants can be pinched back to increase bushiness, and older plants can be disbudded to a few flower buds to produce one or a few large flowers per stem.

Among other techniques for propagation is the development of cuttings removed from the midsection of vigorous stems. In spring, take only three cuttings per healthy plant to avoid weakening the mother plant. Root the cuttings in sand, then plant them in well-drained garden soil in a sunny area. Late summer cuttings can be used to develop plants for the coming year but must be protected from heavy frost and poor drainage if they are to survive the winter season.

Clumps of carnations can be lifted and placed in a greenhouse or cool storage area. Those that survive the winter can be divided in spring to produce more garden plants.

Excellent strains of the carnation include Chabaud Hybrids, Grenadins, and Marguerites, all of which are near the size and growth of florist carnations. These larger varieties may also be listed as Super Giants, Chabaud Giants, and English Giants. Excellent dwarf strains include Dwarf Vienna and Juliet Hybrid. These plants need no staking.

Unfortunately, because carnations are of reasonable price and are sometimes artificially colored, people have the false impression that they are inferior flowers. As cut flowers, however, they are unequalled. Few garden perennials provide such fragrance and delightful color patterns, as well as continuous bloom. And, like the mothers they have been chosen to honor, their strength and reliability are unmatched.

Harold W. Rock

I Remember When . . .
May Day Was Spring's Social Highlight

Adeline Roseberg

When we were young, we didn't hang May baskets on just the first day of May. No, we hung May baskets throughout the month of May—it was the social highlight of our group of kids and a delightful way to spend fine spring evenings.

But anticipating and preparing for our month-long celebration of May Day was half the fun. We'd spend hours on end making our May baskets out of boxes that we had saved because they seemed to be just the right size and shape. Then we'd sew strips of cardboard onto the baskets to serve as handles and cover them with fancy wallpaper from sample books, pretty pictures we had cut out of magazines or with brightly-colored crepe paper.

When May arrived, we prevailed on older sisters and Mother to bake cookies and make candies to put into the baskets. For last-minute additions, it wasn't hard to find mayflowers, violets and trilliums.

During the day, we hung May baskets for our grandmothers and shut-ins, mostly at the prompting of our parents. We'd hang the May basket on the doorknob and slip away quietly, later to hear how much the pleasant surprise had been appreciated.

Catching the "Hangers"

But the great fun—as far as we kids were concerned—came in the evening. I can still remember sitting around after dinner just reading or talking, to suddenly hear a loud bang on the door. We'd rush to open the door, trying to catch sight of who had hung the May basket. Usually, whoever it was was already off hiding.

So we'd pick up the basket and bring it in, with each of us kids reaching in for a piece of candy or a fancy cookie before we went dashing back out the door again to try to catch the "hangers." We'd look behind the house, around the sheds and barn, in the bushes, and sometimes even up a tree before we'd finally find all our friends.

Then we'd thank our friends for the May basket and invite them in the house for refreshments and games. There were always big glasses of cold milk and maybe big sugar cookies, pieces of molasses cake or maybe just thick slices of homemade rye bread with plenty of butter. Whatever the treat was, it surely tasted good after we had done all that running around.

Games followed next on the agenda of the night's events. We'd play bean bag toss or hide-the-thimble until it was time for our guests to go home. Then it was just part of the tradition to follow them halfway home.

The next evening or sometime soon, we'd repay those same neighbor children by hanging a May basket at their house. Again, we'd follow pretty much the same procedure of eating cookies and playing games.

At the same time, we'd make plans with them to all go to someone else's house on another evening. That gave us still something else to look forward to and plan for.

On the evenings that we were home, we'd always hope to hear another knock at our door, for hanging May baskets and receiving them was exciting. And that's the way we continued to celebrate all the merry month of May.

The mother is a gardener,
Planting the seeds
Of faith, truth, and love
That develop into the fairest flowers
Of character, virtue, and happiness
In the lives of her children.

J. Harold Gwynne

My Mother's Garden

Today, in thinking, suddenly I knew
The secret of her garden and its ways,
Why all the curly roots made haste and grew
And were the first to start their blossom days.

Her pinks would hurry into spicy growing
While still the iris purpled lovely banners;
And past the time for poppies to be going
The petals quite forgot their garden manners.

For I remember how she used to talk
To pansies that looked up with childlike faces;
She knelt to touch them by the garden walk
And all their beauty took on added graces.

Now this one thing at last I surely know:
Flowers, like children, must have love to grow.

Jessie Goddard Broman

My Mother's House

Mary Shirley Krouse

My mother's house has always seemed enchanted,
Perhaps because I've never known the rooms
To echo any sound but gentle music,
Or be without a bowl of garden blooms.

Perhaps because the doors are always open
To welcome anyone who passes by.
Perhaps because the kitchen's never lonely
For homemade bread or apple pie.

Perhaps because the windows always glisten,
And let the warm, sweet sunshine twinkle through;
Perhaps my mother's gracious way of living
These years has made her house enchanted, too.

SHOSHONE "SACAJAWEA"

"Indomitable Spirit,
I was born
on the prairie
with only my shadow
between the sky
and the horizon."

"Sacajawea" (pronounced "Sak-uh-guh-WEE-uh") in Shoshone means "Bird Woman." A member of the Shoshone tribe, Sacajawea grew up in the Yellowstone country of Montana.

She was sold in 1803 to Toussaint Charbonneau, a fur trader and a member of the survey crew which laid out and established the town of Stephensport. In the spring of 1804, Sacajawea and Charbonneau were married in St. Louis and were employed as guides (Charbonneau also served as interpreter) for the Lewis and Clark Expedition to the Pacific Northwest.

Sacajawea gave birth to a son, John Baptiste, less than two months before she departed with the American expedition for the distant Pacific. Throughout twenty months and five thousand miles, the staunch Shoshone girl shared the trials and the trail with the thirty-one men of the expedition. Despite the child on her back, she loyally performed her portion of camp and trail duties. In addition, she helped stave off starvation in the mountains by finding edible roots. Her mere presence prevented attacks by Indians, for a "woman with a party of men is a token of peace," as Clark noted.

This sixteen-year-old girl, courageously carrying her infant, made the five-thousand-mile trip by canoe and portage. En route she was twice a heroine: once, when a canoe overturned and she rescued the expedition's records at the risk of her life, and again in hostile country when her recognition of her brother among approaching Indians enabled the expedition to obtain necessary food and guides.

Sacajawea is especially memorable for having refused to leave her newly-born son behind at the expedition's start. The young Indian's tender ministrations to her infant during the expedition's five thousand-mile trip through the northwest's most rugged country lends her the infinite grace of an "American Madonna."

Sacajawea won everlasting fame for her service to the young and growing United States. More statues have been erected to her memory than to any other woman in American history. A river, a peak and a mountain pass have been given her name. Each year a festival is held in Cloverport, Kentucky, in her honor.

The sculpture "Sacajawea" is part of the Cybis North American Indian Series. It pays tribute to the courage and loyalty that played such an important part in the success of the Lewis and Clark Expedition.

"Sacajawea" is sculpted holding her infant with a basket of some of the sacred plants of the Shoshone tribe—corn, squash and beans—by her side. The colors chosen for the sculpture also held important meaning for the Indians. White symbolized the East; yellow, the West and the sacred pollen. Black represented the North and was considered to be the male color, while blue represented the South and was the female color.

Cybis

My Mother

Minnie Klemme

My mother was a mountain girl;
The mountain stars are in her eyes.
She lived another age and clime,
Beneath another sun and skies.

The forests of her native land
Still hold her as an ancient scroll.
The linnet and the nightingale
Still sing the music of her soul.

The Danube and the Rhine still flow
In their accustomed steady way,
While on the terraces still green
The vineyards of another day.

I wonder oft what memories hold
Of school days when she was a girl:
The village church, the castle walls,
Seeing her country's flag unfurled.

My mother seems to be content;
Perhaps she found the honeycomb.
For all, she smiles and proudly claims,
"America, my home sweet home!"

The Legend of Sally Lunn

Sally Lunn, according to legend, was born and reared in the city of Bath, England, where, in the 1790s, she sold hot tea buns. Some claim Sally was the original maker and inventor of the cakes that bear her name; others, that she had a tea shop of her own. But the most common version of the story is that Sally piled her buns high in a basket, covered them with a linen cloth, and hawked them up and down the streets of the fashionable old watering town.

One day a baker named Dalmer observed that the rich and pampered residents of Bath always bought Sally's cakes. Dalmer, who was a shrewd tradesman, soon realized that here was the germ of a fine business, based on a fine product and a popular personality. So the baker bought out the huckster, named her cakes "Sally Lunns," and—being something of a rhymester and musician as well as a baker—wrote a song about her. The song became popular. Before long everyone in Bath, from butcher boys to gouty old lords who had come for a cure, was humming the new tune. Soon Dalmer's business became so large he needed special barrows to distribute his wares.

Sally Lunns were the sensation of the moment. History says Dalmer rolled up a neat fortune, and a few years later he retired. Regrettably, there is no further mention of Sally. We only hope that her charm and personality won a rich and appreciative husband who doted on Sally and liked hot cakes for tea.

Sally Lunns were the fashion of eighteenth- and nineteenth-century England and their popularity has never entirely waned. English literature abounds in allusions to them. One of the earliest appeared in the *Gentleman's Magazine* for 1798 and refers to "a certain sort of hot rolls now, or not long ago, in vogue at Bath ... gratefully and emphatically styled 'Sally Lunns.'"

Both Carlyle and Dickens—who evidently ate Sally Lunns with relish—mention them in their writings. "Robinson gives me coffee and Sally Lunns," writes Carlyle, while Charles Dickens says in *The Chimes*, "It's a sort of night that's meant for muffins. Likewise crumpets. Also, Sally Lunns." Thackeray must have associated the small buns with intimate moments because, in *Pendennis*, he describes "a meal of green tea, scandal, hot Sally Lunns, and a little novel reading."

Sally Lunns were in such demand in England that the recipe was brought to America. The early formulas differed vastly from modern recipes. One cookbook, for example, directed the housewife to stir together a half pint of milk, a pound of flour, two eggs, a teaspoon of sugar, an ounce of butter, a teaspoon of salt, and a gill of yeast. She was to set the sponge at night and bake it next morning in a pound cake mold. And if, by mischance, the dough turned sour, the recipe advised the housewife to mix in a teaspoon of soda, dissolved in a little sour milk.

Luckily, today's recipe for Sally Lunns is foolproof and, when followed exactly, leaves nothing to chance.

Dorothy Gladys Spicer

Baking Powder SALLY LUNN

2¼ c. flour
1 t. salt
2 T. sugar
4 t. baking powder
⅓ c. butter
3 eggs, separated
1 c. milk

Sift the dry ingredients three times. Cut the butter into the dry ingredients as for pastry. Beat the egg yolks thoroughly and add the milk. Stir into the dry ingredients. Beat egg whites until stiff and fold into mixture. Pour batter into buttered muffin tins. Bake at 400° for 30 minutes or until golden brown. If muffins begin to brown too quickly, cover with aluminum foil.

Darlene Kronschnabel

Yeast SALLY LUNN

⅓ c. sugar
½ c. butter
2 t. salt
1 c. milk, scalded and cooled
1½ pkgs. active dry yeast
¼ c. lukewarm water
3 medium eggs, beaten
4 c. flour

Cream the butter, sugar and salt. Add the cooled milk. Dissolve the yeast in the water and add to the creamed mixture along with the beaten eggs. Add the flour a little at a time, beating well after each addition. Cover and let rise until doubled. Then punch down and pour into a well-greased bundt, loaf or 10-inch angel food cake pan. Cover and let rise again. Bake in a 350° oven for about 40 minutes or until the bread is golden brown and tests done. Bread is done if loaf sounds hollow when lightly tapped.

Darlene Kronschnabel

North Woods Notebook
Memories of My Mother

Bea Bourgeois

My husband, Bob, was the youngest of ten children born to Comb and Anna Andersen Bourgeois. The family lived in Park Falls, Wisconsin, when Bob was born on August 20, 1923; during his childhood there were several moves to farms and small towns throughout northern Wisconsin.

Bob's memories of his childhood remain vivid. When he talks about those distant days, the memories come alive; they are echoes of a way of life that has all but disappeared from the American scene. Here, in this third article, he shares with us treasured remembrances of his mother.

My Mother, Anna Johanna Andersen, was born in Ogema, Wisconsin, in 1882. She was only sixty-four years old when she died in 1946. During her lifetime, she raised ten children during some perilous economic times. She knew the deep joys of mothering such a large family, and she knew the terrible grief that came when two of her children predeceased her.

Being the youngest child, I suppose I naturally felt close to my Mother. When I was in seventh grade, the class was told to make a gift for Mother's Day. I found a heavy piece of posterboard and printed "MOTHER" at the top. Because she loved flowers, I drew several red and yellow roses along the left side of the picture, and in the middle I printed an original poem:

Of all the mothers I have seen,
Or ever can recall,
You are the nicest, and the dearest,
Of them all.

I tried to draw a picture of her, but it wouldn't turn out; finally, in desperation, I asked my friend Don Joanis to draw it for me. The result was a figure that looked like a young Southern Belle in a fancy evening dress with a ribbon in her hair—not remotely resembling my mother! Nevertheless, she loved the picture. I had put a piece of glass on the front, and "framed" the gift with black electrician's tape. She hung it on the wall as soon as she had unwrapped it, and she often told me how much it meant to her.

We were living in Washburn during the summer following my graduation from eighth grade, and I spent a lot of time swimming in Lake Superior. On one burning hot day, before I went to the beach, Ma gave me a penny for a treat. I stopped at the little wooden grocery store and bought two round, pink chunks of bubble gum—sheer delight and something I didn't get very often.

I began to feel peculiar while I was swimming, and I remember that the sweetness of the gum made me feel even sicker. I started walking home, and at some point I fainted on the sidewalk. A neighbor carried me home, and Ma called the doctor.

The diagnosis was diphtheria. The doctor gave me an injection in my back, and when I woke up the bubble gum was stuck in a glob in my right hand; I must have tried to save it. Ma had to use lard to get all the sticky mass off my hand.

For several weeks that summer, the house was quarantined. I couldn't go outside, and none of my friends could come in to play. I read every Big-Little Book I could get my hands on, but Ma knew I was bored and restless. That summer she taught me to embroider, and how to make things out of newspaper. To this day I can make a Jacob's Ladder or a bow tie or a respectable tree out of folded newspaper.

Ma worried a lot about me that summer, and I worried about her. For years she had been troubled with varicose ulcers on her right leg, and there didn't seem to be any cure in those days before penicillin. Her leg always seemed to be more painful in the warm weather, and I worried about her caring for me when I should have been helping her.

Ma was no stranger to worry, anyway; she was the one who worried about the garden, fearful that a bad year would mean a shortage of food the next winter. I remember how discouraged she was during the Depression, when Dad was out of work and there was virtually no money coming in. Once we had potato soup three nights in a row, because potatoes were the only food she had to cook with.

She had many simple pleasures in her life. The radio was her delight, and she followed all the soap operas, although "Ma Perkins" was her favorite. I think my brother Ed and I, and my sister Irene, inherited our love of flowers from Ma; she always managed to keep geraniums blooming in the house all winter long.

Ma loved to dance, too, especially the polka, the waltz, and the circle two-step. She loved to see people have a good time, and on many a Saturday night our living room was filled with family and friends. Ma and Dad would roll up the rug to make a dance floor, and someone would play an accordion or a mandolin. My brother Milt is a self-taught musician who can do just about anything on the guitar, and I'll bet he inherited his love of music from Ma.

A simple deck of playing cards provided endless hours of diversion for my family, and Ma loved a good game of cribbage or five hundred. When her friends came over for an evening of five hundred, she'd wrap up little trinkets as prizes for the highest score and a booby prize for the lowest score. Dad was an excellent cribbage player, and he loved to tease Ma when they played because she so seldom won the game. When she would shuffle the cards too many times, Dad would reprimand her: "Come on and deal, Ma, or you'll shuffle the spots right off the cards."

One of my most painful memories is the day I left home for Fort Sheridan, Illinois, after being drafted to the Army in 1943. My mother wrote to me faithfully every other day, during the three years I was in the service. When I ended up in Calcutta, India, she was sure she would never see me again. Her letters made

me happy and sad at the same time—happy to have news of home, but sad to read when she wrote, "I thought of you last Sunday and wished you could have been here. I made your favorite chicken dinner."

We wrote back and forth about what we would do when I was discharged. Our great dream was to travel to the Black Hills in South Dakota, where Ma and Dad had lived as newlyweds when Dad worked in the mica mines. Unfortunately, our dream never came true. I was discharged in May of 1946, and Ma died the next October. The doctors had started treating her leg condition with sulfa drugs, and discovered too late that she was allergic to sulfa. Her reaction led to the uremic poisoning that was the ultimate cause of her death.

She was truly an unforgettable human being, and she still lives in my memories. I think we were all awfully lucky to have her for our mother.

Memories

Helen Shick

A home is a place
Where memories weave
A pattern untouched
By what time may achieve.

A home holds sweet memories:
A footstep, a cry,
A touch to the walls,
Or an echo, a sigh.

It's a place full of riches
Time cannot destroy;
It's a hall of remembrance
For each girl and boy.
A home is a place
That holds many things:
Like wonderful dreams
Left from yesterday's flings.

It holds every sound
With love in its walls:
Like the murmur of children,
Their shouts and their calls.

It treasures sweet memories,
The foundation is blessed;
And it stands in the world,
A true haven of rest.

Love Is a Guest

Irene Taylor

There is children's happy laughter,
There's a watchful mother, too,
There are climbing morning glories,
Cool and fresh, and wet with dew.

There's a puppy and a kitten,
Trees to dapple-shade a yard;
There's a swing, a bike and clutter;
There are porch steps, worn and scarred.

There's a pan of cookies baking,
There's a cooling apple pie,
There's a cheery, "Well, good morning,"
When the postman passes by.

Walk carefully near the lilacs;
There's a thrush there on her nest.
Oh, home is where the heart is
When love's a constant guest.

Mother

I think God took the fragrance
Of a flower,
A flower, which blooms
Not for world praise
But which makes sweet and beautiful some bower;
The compassion of the dew,
Which gently lays
Reviving freshness on the fainting earth,
And gives to all the tired things
New birth;
The steadfastness and radiance of stars
Which lift the soul above confining bars;
The gladness of fair dawns;
The sunset's peace;
Contentment which from trivial rounds
Asks no release;
The life which finds its greatest joy
In deeds of love for others.
I think God took these precious things
And made of them mothers.

Author Unknown

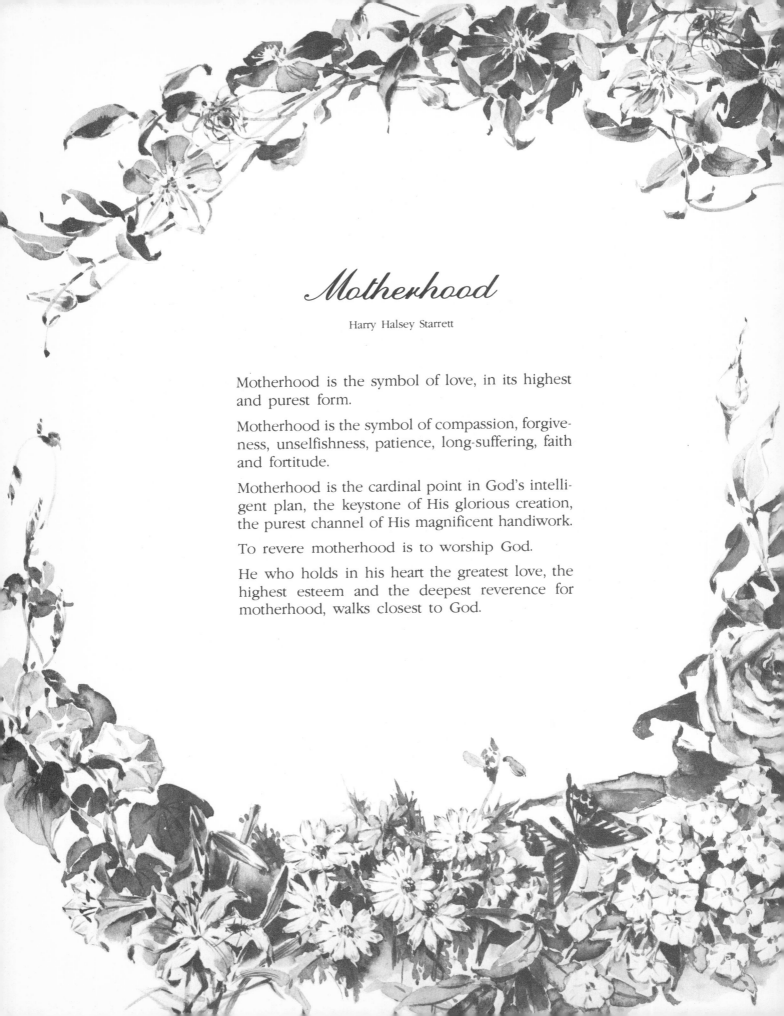

Motherhood

Harry Halsey Starrett

Motherhood is the symbol of love, in its highest and purest form.

Motherhood is the symbol of compassion, forgiveness, unselfishness, patience, long-suffering, faith and fortitude.

Motherhood is the cardinal point in God's intelligent plan, the keystone of His glorious creation, the purest channel of His magnificent handiwork.

To revere motherhood is to worship God.

He who holds in his heart the greatest love, the highest esteem and the deepest reverence for motherhood, walks closest to God.

A Mother's Prayer

Ruth Tubia

On this Mother's Day and every day let me remember my responsibilities rather than my privileges as a mother . . .

Let me be wise enough to love my children without possessing them.

Let me be wise enough to earn their respect, not demand it.

Let me be as understanding and patient with their mistakes as I am with my own.

Above all, let me remember that these children of God have been graciously loaned to me so that together we may find the Christ in one another.

Let me be thankful every moment of every day for this responsibility . . . a chance to serve others and to grow.

Little Women

Louisa May Alcott

Written in 1868, *Little Women* has earned worldwide recognition as a warm and touching novel for children as well as adults. Louisa May Alcott based the characters on her own family, though the events surrounding the March family were not similar. The story, though written over one hundred years ago, develops the familiar theme of growing up that applies as much to children today as to those of earlier generations. In this chapter, the March sisters try a week-long experiment of doing nothing but having fun. Mrs. March, with a mother's innate feeling for what is best, leaves the girls to their own devices. This excerpt gives the reader a glimpse of the special relationship between mothers and daughters. The story is written in a sensitive and loving manner which will leave you with a desire to read more.

"The first of June! The Kings are off to the seashore tomorrow, and I'm free. Three months' vacation—how I shall enjoy it!" exclaimed Meg, coming home one warm day to find Jo laid upon the sofa in an unusual state of exhaustion, while Beth took off her dusty boots, and Amy made lemonade for the refreshment of the whole party. . . .

"What shall you do all your vacation?" asked Amy. . . .

"I shall lie abed late and do nothing," replied Meg, from the depths of the rocking chair. "I've been routed up early all winter and had to spend my days working for other people; so now I'm going to rest and revel to my heart's content."

"No," said Jo, "that dozy way wouldn't suit me. I've laid in a heap of books, and I'm going to improve my shining hours reading on my perch in the old apple tree, when I'm not having larks." . . .

"Don't let us do any lessons, Beth, for a while, but play all the time, and rest, as the girls mean to," proposed Amy.

"Well, I will, if mother doesn't mind. I want to learn some new songs, and my children need fitting up for the summer; they are dreadfully out of order, and really suffering for clothes."

"May we, mother?" asked Meg, turning to Mrs. March, who sat sewing, in what they called "Marmee's corner."

"You may try your experiment for a week and see how you like it. I think by Saturday night you will find that all play and no work is as bad as all work and no play."

"Oh, dear, no! It will be delicious, I'm sure," said Meg complacently.

"I now propose a toast, as my 'friend and pardner, Sairy Gamp,' says, 'Fun forever, and no grubbing!'" cried Jo, rising, glass in hand, as the lemonade went round.

They all drank it merrily and began the experiment by lounging for the rest of the day. Next morning, Meg did not appear till ten o'clock; her solitary breakfast did not taste nice, and the room seemed lonely and untidy; for Jo had not filled the vases, Beth had not dusted, and Amy's books lay scattered about. Nothing was neat and pleasant but "Marmee's corner," which looked as usual; and there Meg sat, to "rest and read," which meant yawn, and imagine what pretty summer dresses she would get with her salary. Jo spent the morning on the river, with Laurie, and the afternoon reading and crying over "The Wide, Wide World," up in the apple tree. Beth began by rummaging everything out of the big closet, where her family resided; but, getting tired before half done, she left her establishment topsy-turvy, and went to her music, rejoicing that she had no dishes to wash. Amy arranged her bower, put on her best white frock, smoothed her curls, and sat down to draw, under the honeysuckles, hoping someone would see and inquire who the young artist was. As no one appeared but an inquisitive daddy longlegs, who examined her work with interest, she went to walk, got caught in a shower, and came home dripping.

At teatime they compared notes, and all agreed that it had been a delightful, though unusually long, day. Meg, who went shopping in the afternoon and got a "sweet blue muslin," had discovered, after she had cut the breadths off, that it wouldn't wash, which mishap made her slightly cross. Jo had burnt the skin off her nose boating, and got a raging headache by reading too long. Beth was worried by the confusion of her closet, and the difficulty of learning three or four songs at once; and Amy deeply regretted the damage done her frock. . . . But these were mere trifles; and they assured their mother that the experiment was working finely. She smiled, said nothing, and, with Hannah's help, did their neglected work, keeping home pleasant, and the domestic machinery running smoothly. . . .

No one would own that they were tired of the experiment; but, by Friday night, each acknowledged to herself that she was glad the week was nearly done. Hoping to impress the lesson more deeply, Mrs. March, who had a good deal of humor, resolved to finish off the trial in an

continued

appropriate manner; so she gave Hannah a holiday, and let the girls enjoy the full effect of the play system.

When they got up on Saturday morning, there was no fire in the kitchen, no breakfast in the dining room, and no mother anywhere to be seen.

"Mercy on us! What *has* happened?" cried Jo, staring about her in dismay.

Meg ran upstairs, and soon came back again, looking relieved, but rather bewildered, and a little ashamed.

"Mother isn't sick, only very tired, and she says she is going to stay quietly in her room all day, and let us do the best we can. It's a very queer thing for her to do; she doesn't act a bit like herself, but she says it has been a hard week for her, so we mustn't grumble, but take care of ourselves."

"That's easy enough, and I like the idea; I'm aching for something to do—that is, some new amusement, you know," added Jo quickly.

In fact it *was* an immense relief to them all to have a little work, and they took hold with a will, but soon realized the truth of Hannah's saying, "Housekeeping ain't no joke." There was plenty of food in the larder, and, while Beth and Amy set the table, Meg and Jo got breakfast, wondering, as they did so, why servants ever talked about hard work.

"I shall take some up to mother, though she said we were not to think of her, for she'd take care of herself," said Meg, who presided, and felt quite matronly behind the teapot.

So a tray was fitted out before any one began, and taken up, with the cook's compliments. The boiled tea was very bitter, the omelette scorched, and the biscuits speckled with saleratus; but Mrs. March received her repast with thanks, and laughed heartily over it after Meg was gone.

"Poor little souls, they will have a hard time, I'm afraid; but they won't suffer, and it will do them good," she said, producing the more palatable viands with which she had provided herself, and disposing of the bad breakfast, so that their feelings might not be hurt—a motherly little deception, for which they were grateful.

Many were the complaints below, and great the chagrin of the head cook at her failures. "Never mind, I'll get the dinner, and be servant; you be mistress, keep your hands nice, see company, and give orders," said Jo, who knew still less than Meg about culinary affairs.

This obliging offer was gladly accepted; and Margaret retired to the parlor, which she hastily put in order by whisking the litter under the sofa, and shutting the blinds, to save the trouble of dusting. Jo, with perfect faith in her own powers, ... immediately put a note in the office, inviting Laurie to dinner.

"You'd better see what you have got before you think of having company," said Meg, when informed of the hospitable but rash act.

"Oh, there's corned beef and plenty of potatoes; and I shall get some asparagus, and a lobster, 'for a relish,' as

Hannah says. We'll have lettuce, and make a salad. I don't know how, but the book tells. I'll have blancmange and strawberries for dessert; and coffee, too, if you want to be elegant."

"Don't try too many messes, Jo, for you can't make anything but gingerbread and molasses candy fit to eat. I wash my hands of the dinner party; and, since you have asked Laurie on your own responsibility, you may just take care of him."

"I don't want you to do anything but be civil to him, and help with the pudding. You'll give me your advice if I get in a muddle, won't you?" asked Jo, rather hurt.

"Yes, but I don't know much, except about bread, and a few trifles. You had better ask mother's leave before you order anything," returned Meg prudently.

"Of course I shall; I'm not a fool," and Jo went off in a huff at the doubts expressed of her power.

"Get what you like, and don't disturb me; I'm going out to dinner, and can't worry about things at home," said Mrs. March, when Jo spoke to her. "I never enjoyed housekeeping, and I'm going to take a vacation today, and read, write, go visiting, and amuse myself."

The unusual spectacle of her busy mother rocking comfortably, and reading, early in the morning, made Jo feel as if some natural phenomenon had occurred, for an eclipse, an earthquake, or a volcanic eruption would hardly have seemed stranger. . . .

"Here's a sweet prospect!" muttered Jo, slamming the stove door open, and poking vigorously among the cinders.

Having rekindled the fire, she thought she would go to market while the water heated. The walk revived her spirits; and, flattering herself that she had made good bargains, she trudged home again, after buying a very young lobster, some very old asparagus, and two boxes of acid strawberries. By the time she got cleared up, the dinner arrived, and the stove was red hot. Hannah had left a pan of bread to rise, Meg had worked it up early, set it on the hearth for a second rising, and forgotten it. Meg was entertaining Sallie Gardiner in the parlor, when the door flew open, and a floury, crocky, flushed, and dishevelled figure appeared, demanding tartly:

"I say, isn't bread 'riz' enough when it runs over the pans?"

Sallie began to laugh; but Meg nodded, and lifted her eyebrows as high as they would go, which caused the apparition to vanish, and put the sour bread into the oven without further delay. Mrs. March went out, after peeping here and there to see how matters went. . . . A strange sense of helplessness fell upon the girls as the gray bonnet vanished round the corner; and despair seized them, when, a few minutes later, Miss Crocker appeared, and said she'd come to dinner. Now, this lady was a thin, yellow spinster, with a sharp nose and inquisitive eyes, who saw everything, and gossiped about all she saw. . . . Meg gave her the easy chair, and tried to entertain her, while she asked questions, criticized everything, and told stories of the people whom she knew.

Language cannot describe the anxieties, experiences and exertions which Jo underwent that morning; and the dinner she served up became a standing joke. Fearing to ask any more advice, she did her best alone and discovered that something more than energy and goodwill is necessary to make a cook. She boiled the asparagus for an hour and was grieved to find the heads cooked off and the stalks harder than ever. The bread burnt black, for the salad dressing so aggravated her that she let everything else go till she had convinced herself that she could not make it fit to eat. The lobster was a scarlet mystery to her, but she hammered and poked till it was unshelled and its meagre proportions concealed in a grove of lettuce leaves. The potatoes had to be hurried, not to keep the asparagus waiting, and were not done at last. The blancmange was lumpy, and the strawberries not as ripe as they looked, having been skillfully "deaconed." ...

Jo's one strong point was the fruit, for she had sugared it well, and had a pitcher of rich cream to eat with it. Her hot cheeks cooled a trifle, and she drew a long breath, as the pretty glass plates went round, and every one looked graciously at the little rosy islands floating in a sea of cream. Miss Crocker tasted first, made a wry face, and drank some water hastily. Jo, who had refused, thinking there might not be enough, for they dwindled sadly after the picking over, glanced at Laurie, but he was eating away manfully, though there was a slight pucker about his mouth, and he kept his eye fixed on his plate. Amy, who was fond of delicate fare, took a heaping spoonful, choked, hid her face in her napkin, and left the table precipitately.

"Oh, what is it?" exclaimed Jo trembling.

"Salt instead of sugar, and the cream is sour," replied Meg, with a tragic gesture.

Jo uttered a groan, and fell back in her chair, remembering that she had given a last hasty powdering to the berries out of one of the two boxes on the kitchen table, and had neglected to put the milk in the refrigerator. She turned scarlet and was on the verge of crying, when she met Laurie's eyes, which would look merry in spite of his heroic efforts; the comical side of the affair suddenly struck her, and she laughed till the tears ran down her cheeks. So did every one else, even "Croaker," as the girls called the old lady; and the unfortunate dinner ended gaily, with bread and butter, olives and fun. ...

Meg helped Jo clear away the remains of the feast, which took half the afternoon, and left them so tired that they agreed to be contented with tea and toast for supper. ... Mrs. March came home to find the three older girls hard at work in the middle of the afternoon; and a glance at the closet gave her an idea of the success of one part of the experiment.

Before the housewives could rest, several people called, and there was a scramble to get ready to see them; then tea must be got, errands done; and one or two necessary bits of sewing neglected till the last minute. As twilight fell, dewy and still, one by one they gathered in the porch where the June roses were budding beautifully, and each groaned or sighed as she sat down, as if tired or troubled.

"What a dreadful day this has been!" began Jo, usually the first to speak.

"It has seemed shorter than usual, but *so* uncomfortable," said Meg.

"Not a bit like home," added Amy. ...

As she spoke, Mrs. March came and took her place among them, looking as if her holiday had not been much pleasanter than theirs.

"Are you satisfied with your experiment, girls, or do you want another week of it?" she asked, as Beth nestled up to her, and the rest turned toward her with brightening faces, as flowers turn toward the sun.

"I don't!" cried Jo decidedly.

"Nor I," echoed the others.

"You think, then, that it is better to have a few duties, and live a little for others, do you?"

"Lounging and larking doesn't pay," observed Jo, shaking her head. "I'm tired of it and mean to go to work at something right off."

"Suppose you learn plain cooking; that's a useful accomplishment, which no woman should be without," said Mrs. March, laughing inaudibly at the recollection of Jo's dinner party; for she had met Miss Crocker, and heard her account of it.

"Mother, did you go away and let everything be, just to see how we'd get on?" cried Meg, who had had suspicions all day.

"Yes; I wanted you to see how the comfort of all depends on each doing her share faithfully. While Hannah and I did your work, you got on pretty well, though I don't think you were very happy or amiable; so I thought, as a little lesson, I would show you what happens when everyone thinks only of herself. Don't you feel that it is pleasanter to help one another, to have daily duties which make leisure sweet when it comes, and to bear and forbear, that home may be comfortable and lovely to us all?"

"We do, mother, we do!" cried the girls.

"Then let me advise you to take up your little burdens again; for though they seem heavy sometimes, they are good for us, and lighten as we learn to carry them. Work is wholesome, and there is plenty for everyone; it keeps us from *ennui* and mischief, is good for health and spirits, and gives us a sense of power and independence better than money or fashion."

"We'll work like bees, and love it too; see if we don't!" said Jo. ...

"Very good! Then I am quite satisfied with the experiment, and fancy that we shall not have to repeat it; only don't go to the other extreme, and delve like slaves. Have regular hours for work and play; make each day both useful and pleasant, and prove that you understand the worth of time by employing it well. Then youth will be delightful, old age will bring few regrets, and life become a beautiful success, in spite of poverty."

"We'll remember, mother!" and they did.

God's Gifts

God created beauty
When He created flowers
And sprinkled them profusely
Upon this earth of ours.

Each blossom is a token
Of love beyond compare,
A tender language of the heart
For everyone to share.

And have you ever noticed,
With a special kind of grace,
How like the loveliest
Flower that grows
Is a mother's gentle face?

Nadine Brothers Lybarger

God's Garden

When the wise God planted His garden,
Scattering the seeds from above,
The choicest seed in His packet
Was the flower of mother love.

Carefully watched over and tended,
Nurtured by sunshine and shower,
Ever growing sturdy and stronger,
It blooms, a beautiful flower.

A flower so sweet and entrancing,
Dazzling and shining and white,
A love that guards us and guides us
Through life, our beacon light.

A love that steadies our footsteps,
That stretches a helpful hand,
That comforts our sorrows and heartaches,
That always will understand.

Mother love ... God's gift to His children,
With heavenly fragrance fraught,
The brightest flower in God's garden,
His truest forget-me-not.

Myrtie Fisher Seaverns

Known as the "First Lady of the American Theater," Helen Hayes has enjoyed an extended career both on Broadway and in movies. Her career, supported by her mother, began in 1905 at age five with a stage debut in Washington, D.C. It wasn't until 1918, however, that Miss Hayes drew public attention at the age of eighteen for her role in *Dear Brutus*. Over the years, the American people have witnessed the wide range of her performing ability. Not wishing to be stereotyped into roles of "sunshine and lace," Miss Hayes also brought her talents to the portrayal of highly emotional and dramatically forceful characters. She was awarded the Oscar for *The Sin of Madelon Claudet* (1931) and *Airport* (1971). Along with two Oscars, she received the Tony Award for *Time Remembered* (1958). The plays in which she has appeared include *Victoria Regina* (1935), *The Glass Menagerie* (1948), *What Every Woman Knows* (1926, 1954), and *A Touch of the Poet* (1958). Her thirty-year marriage to Charles MacArthur was filled with much love and happiness, and both parents were deeply committed to their daughter and son. Though still active in charity work, Miss Hayes enjoys spending time with her grandchildren. A personal view of Helen Hayes may be found in the following letter to those grandchildren.

My Dear Grandchildren

Helen Hayes

At this writing, it is no longer fashionable to have faith; but your grandmother has never been famous for her chic, so she isn't bothered by the intellectual hemlines. I have always been concerned with the whole, not the fragments; the positive, not the negative; the words, not the spaces between them. I loved and married my Charlie, your grandfather, because he was both poem and poet. What wonders he could work with words.

From your parents you learn love and laughter and how to put one foot before another. But when books are opened you discover that you have wings.

No one can tell me that man's presence on earth isn't expected—even announced. Because the magi come to each new babe and offer up such treasures as to dazzle the imagination. For what are jewels and spices and caskets of gold when compared with the minds and hearts of great men?

What can a grandmother offer in the midst of such plenty? I wondered. With the feast of millenia set before you, the saga of all mankind on your bookshelf, what could I give you, Jim's children? And then I knew. Of course. My own small footnote. The homemade bread at the banquet. The private joke in the divine comedy. Your roots.

This, then, is the grandmother's special gift: a bridge to your past. It goes back, of course, to the beginning of time, but I cannot give it substance until my entrance. After all, I am the star.

I arrived with the century but, like the rest of man's history, mine begins with the fall. I arrived—Helen Hayes Brown did—on the tenth of October, 1900, in Washington, D.C. Center stage, of course. Part of the first harvest, I was in plenty of time for Thanksgiving; and looking back on a lifetime filled with the usual quota of pain and guilt and might-have-been, I still offer up a loud hosanna. It's been marvelous. Yes. I came with the century and I believe always in leaving with my escort. It would be nice if it can be managed. I don't want to miss a thing.

Heaven knows my life hasn't always been wise and faultless. It is a pastiche made up of opposites, of lethargy and bossiness, of pride and guilt, of discipline and frivolity. It hasn't always been a model and worthy of imitation, but it was round and it was real and I lived it all greedily.

Your grandmother is an actress who has spent her working life pretending to be gay or sad, hoping that the audience felt the same. More often than not I succeeded. Offstage, I was not always in such control. The technique of living is far more elusive. Alas! One does her best and, like Thornton Wilder's Mrs. Antrobus, I have survived.

Cast by the fates as Helen Hayes, I have played the part for all it's worth. Child, maiden, sweetheart, wife, and now grandmother. We play many parts in this world and I want you to know them all, for together they make the whole. Trials and errors, hits and misses, I have enjoyed my life, children, and I pray you will, too.

And so—in highlights and shadows, bits and pieces, in recalled moments, mad scenes and acts of folly—all chiaroscuro and confetti—this is what it was like to be me, all the me's; what it was like to live in such exciting times and know so many of the men and women who made it so.

What are little grandchildren made of?
Some good and some bad from Mother and Dad
And laughs and wails and Grandmother's tales.

I love you.

Grammy

For the mother is and must be, whether she knows it or not, the greatest, strongest and most lasting teacher her children have.

Hannah Whitall Smith

Grandmother

She has about her the quality of a summer willow . . .

A pleasantness that seems to say, "Come, sit in my shade and look at the quiet goodness of earth."

She has within her a constancy which never blares or barbs, but speaks to one who listens of His love . . .

Somehow, in her truth, the storm of life becomes the kiss of raindrops.

Shirley Garfin

The Afterglow

Means Hope

Marjorie Holmes

My mother always loved sunsets. This is true of many people, but Mother had a special feeling for them; she kept almost daily appointment with them, and she savored them until the last glow faded from the sky.

We lived in a small Iowa town which boasts a long and lovely lake. And though our house was small, it overlooked a tag end of the water where the sun seemed to fling its gaudiest banners at the end of the day.

"Oh, just look at that sunset!" Mother was always urging. "You can do those dishes later—your lessons can wait." We must stop whatever we were doing to follow her pleased gaze upward. "Isn't that the most beautiful sky you've ever seen?"

She always acted as if a sunset were something new and glorious and amazing, and we must observe it with as much intensity as if no sunset were ever to appear again. And though we often teased her about it, I realize now that those flaming sunsets compensated for many things we lacked during those grim, depressing years. They were her daily luxury.

Later, when the bright hues had melted into the dusk and there was nothing left of the sunset but a last lingering band of burning rose, she would return to the porch a minute and stand there, arms sometimes wrapped in her apron against the chill, and murmur: "The afterglow means hope."

Hope. The afterglow means—hope! ... The boy of your dreams would call ... The test grade would be high ... You'd get that scholarship for college ... The job you wanted so desperately would materialize ... The great, big, wonderful world of love and wealth and achievement would open up to you ... These are the faces of hope when you are young and looking up, eagerly seeking answers in a band of final color across a darkening sky.

As for her, dimly I sensed the meaning of hope to my mother: The problems of all those about her would be resolved ... Wounds would be healed, family frictions smoothed ... The doctor's report on Dad would be favorable ... The company policy would be more generous. There would be enough money to go around ... Her children's often turbulent lives would get straightened out—the boys would find themselves, the girls would marry the right sweethearts—in time they would all be happy and make good.

For while the hooks upon which a youngster hangs his hopes are intensely selfish and personal, those of a mother are multiple; they encompass the entire circle of her family. Her dreams are no longer rooted in self, but in these others.

Yet standing on that porch together long ago, each of us saw in that smoldering band of light a symbol of happier, brighter tomorrows.

Hope. "The afterglow means hope." I don't know whether she had heard the phrase or coined it out of her own indomitable spirit. But I think of it whenever I see the quiet rosy afterlight that follows the blazing sunset. As if a few stubborn coals remain against the coming darkness, little fires of faith that cling long after the sunset is gone.

"The Afterglow Means Hope" from LOVE AND LAUGHTER by Marjorie Holmes, Copyright © 1967 by Marjorie Holmes Mighell. Reprinted by permission of Doubleday & Company, Inc.

There Is No Time
Like Spring

The beauty that God placed on earth
   Is fairest in the spring,
When all the fields and trees turn green
   And birds begin to sing.

It seems as though an artist took
   A palette in his hand
And, with a few deft strokes, erased
   The starkness of the land.

God gave us other seasons, too,
   But none I think so fair,
As that of spring when all the earth
   Is crowned with beauty rare.

Harold F. Mohn

Things Mothers
Love . . .

Mothers love the simple things—
  Soft white lambs that springtime brings,
  Homemade kites in windswept skies,
  Kittens chasing butterflies,
  White sheets tossing in the wind,
  Country roads that turn and bend.

Mothers love the quiet things—
  Fairy tales of knights and kings,
  Swings that sail high in the air,
  Cuddling in a rocking chair,
  Giving children gentle hugs,
  Katydids and ladybugs.

Mothers love the swift things, too—
  Sudden showers passing through,
  White-tailed deer and darting swallow,
  Horses racing in the hollow,
  Lightning cutting jagged ridges,
  Water rushing under bridges.

Mothers love the deeper things—
  Sundays when the church bell rings,
  Moments shared and meals together,
  Fireside glow in stormy weather,
  Hearing prayers when day is done,
  One bright star to wish upon.

Alice Leedy Mason

Dandelion Bouquets

Give me a bunch of little flowers,
The ones that try to hide,
Those dwarfed by brilliant beauties
When they're growing side by side.
I like the scented violets,
The daisies in the grass,
And the baby pansy faces
Peeping shyly as I pass.
I even like the dandelion
With ruffled yellow mane
And frills of golden petals—
You could never call him plain.
Ah! When the family was young
There seldom was a day
When my lounge room wasn't boasting
One bright dandelion bouquet.
At first I'd wrinkle up my nose
With a disgruntled "Phew";
But dandelions in vases
Oddly seem to grow on you,
For it's the flower most often given
In childish love to mother,
And each true home is blessed with it
At one time or another.
You won't preserve it in your fridge
Like orchids from a lover,

And they'll never drop their petals
On a church's altar cover.
You will never see them glowing
In a lovely bride's bouquet;
But they'll bring you wistful memories
Of many a happy day,
For they're the flowers most often given
So lovingly to mother,
And each true home's been blessed with them
At one time or another.

Elsie Pearson

The Poetry of Life

Rose Herriges

Children are the poetry of life, the lyric expression of God's love. Like a poem they are conceived in the rhythm of all beginnings ... the rhythm of life.

They are His song, His creative blessing given to us to enjoy, to guide and to love. Like a poem each is complete in itself and each must be seen, heard and understood to be appreciated.

A poem grows and unfolds according to the understanding of its audience. A child's hidden beauty is ours to discover, to guide into channels designated by inborn qualities.

In children we find the essence of joy, delight and wonder. A child's smile holds all these things and more. It is like a caress from the loving hand of God.

I Am the Child

Mamie Gene Cole

I am the child.
All the world waits for my coming.
And the earth watches with interest
To see what I shall become.
Civilization hangs in the balance,
For what I am
The world of tomorrow will be.

I am the child.
I have come into your world,
About which I knew nothing.
Why I come I know not.
How I came I know not.
I am curious; I am interested.

I am the child.
You hold in your hand my destiny.
You determine, largely,
Whether I shall succeed or fail.
Give me, I pray you, those things
That make for happiness.
Train me, I beg you, that I may be
A blessing to the world.

Morning Vigil

In the early hours of morning
　　When the dew is on the grass
And the earth expectant, silent,
　　Waits for dawning time to pass,
Here I walk my garden pathways
　　Where the fragrant flowers disclose
Secrets of inspiring beauty,
　　Thoughts from mignonette and rose.

Oh, the lovely things they tell me,
　　Silent but true and clear,
And my eager inner spirit
　　Is responsive as I hear
Messages of God's sure bounty,
　　His provision for each need
Of the soul and body hunger . . .
　　Joy flows through me as I heed.

Oh, my garden is God speaking;
　　From this tryst I go forth free
To the duties that are calling,
　　To the work He has for me.
When the tasks seem long and dreary
　　And my spirit is hard-pressed,
I relive the morning vigil,
　　And remembering, I am blest.

Della Adams Leitner

Summer's Message

Out in God's brilliant sunshine
The grass is restful green;
Spirea in the garden shines
With a glimmering sheen.

The birdbath awaits the robins
Who from the treetops fly,
While nearby stands the sundial
Where sunny hours go by.

The rose blooms on the rose vine
Along the garden wall.
Mignonette, her neighbor, sings,
"Miss Rose, I've come to call."

The snowball nods her pretty head
To the peonies, not far away.
And all the flowers hear it said
That summer is here to stay.

Grace Fitzgerald Orr

The *Silence* of a Wood

Patience Strong

Seek the silent woodland,
Where no sound of wheels is heard
And nothing breaks the stillness
Save the singing of a bird.
Nature tells her secrets
Not to those who hurry by,
But to those who walk
With happy heart and seeing eye . . .

The silence of a wood is a living, breathing, speaking
silence. It is full of breath and murmur and flight. The wind
stirs and is a mere sigh in the sentient trees; the sudden
flutter of wings rips at the quiet air and is lost in the muffled
whispering of startled leaves; the sharp snapping of a twig
seems to emphasize the peace which it disturbs; the trill of a
bird sets up a soft ripple of sound upon the surface of
stillness; the sob of doves beats like a pulse at the heart of
the silence.

And in such a silence we can dream our long, slow dreams.
In such a place the heart finds its healing and the spirit
its rest.

The Weaver, May

The weaver, May, before her loom
Began to weave the weather:

For warp and woof she used sunbeams
And songs of birds together.

From out her weft fell drops of pearls
To spangle reeds and rushes,
And then she whisked some silver notes
For morning song of thrushes.

She added hanks of fleecy skies,
All banked with crystal edges,
Threw bolts of yellow daisies down
To trim the roadside hedges.

Her threads of iridescent light
Transformed the hill and heather.

May wound her shuttle with bouquets,
Loosed skeins of golden weather.

Stella Craft Tremble

ACKNOWLEDGMENTS

FACES by Elaine V. Emans. Originally published in SUNDAY SCHOOL CLASSMATE, Cincinnati, Ohio. PORTRAIT OF MY MOTHER (originally titled: MOTHER'S HANDS) by Lydia O. Jackson. Previously published in THE AMERICAN BARD. SALLY LUNN recipes (baking powder and yeast) by Darlene Kronschnabel. From COUNTRY KITCHEN COOKBOOK, Copyright © 1975, Ideals Publishing Corporation. MAY DAY WAS SPRING'S SOCIAL HIGHLIGHT by Adeline Roseberg. Reprinted with permission from FARM WIFE NEWS, P. O. Box 643, Milwaukee, WI 53201. THE WEAVER, MAY by Stella Craft Tremble. From WIND IN THE REED by Stella Craft Tremble. Copyright © 1957 by Bruce Humphries, Inc. Reprinted with permission of the author. THE WATCHER by Margaret Widdemer. From CROSS CURRENTS by Margaret Widdemer. Used with permission of John D. Widdemer. Our sincere thanks to the following authors whose addresses we were unable to locate: Mamie Gene Cole for I AM THE CHILD . . . ; Grace Fitzgerald Orr for SUMMER'S MESSAGE; Dorothy Gladys Spicer for SALLY LUNNS from FEAST-DAY CAKES FROM MANY LANDS by Dorothy Gladys Spicer, Copyright © 1960 by Gladys Spicer Fraser.

COLOR ART AND PHOTO CREDITS
(in order of appearance)

Front and back cover, Colour Library International; inside front and back covers, H. Armstrong Roberts; Mother's love, Three Lions, Inc.; MADAME CAMILLE MONET AND A CHILD IN A GARDEN, Claude Monet, Three Lions, Inc.; Princess Aurora, Cybis Porcelains; Old-fashioned girl, Edgar E. Webber; Rose arbor, Fred Sieb; Beaded fashions, Gerald Koser; Old-fashioned pictures, Gerald Koser; Rhododendron garden, H. Armstrong Roberts; Carnations and lace, Gerald Koser; Greenhouse, Colour Library International; Fragrant baskets, Fred Sieb; Shoshone "Sacajawea," Cybis Porcelains; Sally Lunns, Gerald Koser; Cooking with love, Four By Five, Inc.; Amaryllis blooms, Bob Taylor; FAMILY GROUP, Albert Herter, Three Lions, Inc.; Summer flowers, Colour Library International; Shared moment, Robert Cushman Hayes; Edisto Gardens, Orangeburg, South Carolina, Fred Sieb; Quiet kitten, Colour Library International; Childhood friends, Four By Five, Inc.; Pitcher with basin, Colour Library International; Orton Plantation, North Carolina, Freelance Photographers Guild; Sundial with flowers, Colour Library International; Summer pastels, Fred Sieb.

A Treasured Gift . . .

Our upcoming issue, Friendship Ideals, portrays the lasting values of friendship we all cherish in an outstanding array of poetry, prose and feature articles. The selections are accompanied by beautiful color photography and artwork.

Enjoy a visit with Sherlock Holmes and his friend, Dr. Watson, the ever-popular literary detectives, and their creator, A. Conan Doyle. Learn of the unique features of the Jade Plant and how it got its nickname, the "Friendship" plant. Delight in a child's summertime adventures in "Northwoods Notebook" by Bea Bourgeois. Recapture the glories of yesterday as we take a look at colorful antique movie posters.

Share the beautiful world of Ideals with your family, special friend or favorite relative today and every day of the year. Give a gift subscription beginning with Friendship Ideals and your thoughtfulness will be rewarded with many hours of reading pleasure. Let Ideals say "I'm thinking of you" year-round!